TABLE OF CONTENTS

Self-Enhancement to Leadership
Student Leadership Guide

Introduction

So often we hear before a person can lead they must follow. Although, I believe in this common statement there is one aspect I will focus on. This aspect I will share is self-enhancement. Self is focusing on you as an individual. Self is all decisions that are beneficial to your self-worth. Enhancement is the improvement of yourself or something to become more stable. As individuals, no one is perfect nor will make all the right choices. We must be in the mindset of learning and growing from our mistakes. Two areas that will be covered very much in depth about self-enhancement are marketing (as it relates to oneself) and branding. They contribute a lot to developing self-enhancement.

Why is self-enhancement important? As a person develops in leadership roles, they must first follow others but with a leadership mindset. One must first establish their brand before marketing it. As this book continues you will learn how to use a leadership mindset to your advantage. What I love about having this mindset is it's easy to learn and helpful in many real-life situations. It's so easy to learn I am sure students from middle school up to working adults can implement it. As you grow in the workforce, you must learn to grow in knowledge and skill to improve performance. Performance is the output that determines a success of an individual in a business or corporation.

The true importance of self-enhancement is building your credibility, brand, marketing capabilities, and impact as a person. One of the long-term benefits of self-enhancement is a legacy. Your process in self-enhancement can also be considered as legacy building. Legacy and motivation drive enhancement. The motivation helps to upkeep the vision to reach self-enhancement. In the process of self-enhancement, there is no room for being content. This is one way that leadership growth is limited.

Chapter 1: Self Enhancement

We all want to excel in one thing or another. Self-enhancement is the answer to whatever you want to excel in or achieve. Self-enhancement is dealing with looking deep within and deciding what area in your life can use improvement. It is not a bad thing. Think of self-enhancement as a learning process. For example, some of the greatest cooks did not become the cooks they are overnight. In order for them to reach their fullest potential, they had to learn from others. They had to have the willingness to learn and grow. Self-enhancement is the same way. We are not talking about an overnight process.

Self-enhancement takes time but is effective. Step 1 to self-enhancement is setting three realistic and attainable goals. The reason for setting these goals is to track your process. The goals you are setting are like that outfit you can't fit in but you are passionate you will fit in it again. The purpose of the example is to show there is a process to go through in order to get the desired result. Step 2 in self-enhancement is creating an action plan. It is imperative in fulfilling any goal or objective. The purpose of the action plan is to set up a routine on how you will reach your goal.

You will come to find out that depending on your goal, it may be narrow (short-term) or broad (long-term). An example of a narrow goal is losing 50 pounds. You set up a daily routine for so many hours a day to work out and set up a dietary model to follow. For other goals, the routine and format you will use are broader. For example, starting a business is very broad and requires more planning. In a business startup, there are multiple things you must consider such as startup capital, geographic location, business type product or service, target audience, and so on.

What should be in your action plan? Here are some questions to ask yourself when determining a plan of action.

1. What resources do I have or can obtain to be beneficial to what I want to do?
2. What type of financial services are needed to make it work?
3. When do I want this goal completed?
4. What result do I hope to gain?
5. What is the purpose of the goal?
6. What is your Plan B?

Step 3 is implementation. This process requires dedication. Often times, it is hard to work at something when it does not go your way. Not everything is going to be perfect the first time but keep working on it and keep your eyes on the prize. When children first learn how to ride a bicycle they are going to fall off the first couple times. The most important thing is dusting yourself off, getting back on the bike and not giving up. Nothing is impossible if you put your mind into it. Implementation is putting your action plan in motion. You must be relentless in completing your goal. I also strongly encourage letting your spirituality be your guiding force. Prayer can help in making sure that your direction is clear of all obstacles. The implementation serves as your GPS. It has all the turn by turn directions all you have to do is follow it. At the same time, carry a road map just in case. The road map symbolizes your Plan B. Have set times during each day you will work on your goal(s). Get valuable input or motivation from close friends, family, and spiritual leaders. Remember your results come from the effort put in by you.

Step 4 is stability. How will you maintain your goal? Usually, the largest problem people have is maintaining their goals. The desired result is acquired but then the spirit of content comes about. Being content is a spirit that dwells on you from reaching a goal and being over assured that stability is already present. Even when an individual has a weight loss breakthrough they must still maintain routines and stay active to stabilize their weight. After your goal is reached, ask yourself this question, "What can I do to improve this change in my life?" Change comes with self-enhancement.

Chapter 2: Leadership Mindset

In this book, self-enhancement was mentioned in the first chapter. It affects the way we perceive not only leadership but ourselves. The largest part of self-enhancement in a leadership perspective is having the leadership mindset. It is a thinking process that followers, as well as leaders, can have to increase performance. Very often I see that if you are employed at a company and not in "that desired position" you don't give it your all. That is a very common mindset in a lot of businesses and companies. I have news that common mindset will not get you any further than where you already are. The purpose of this chapter is to enlighten you on why the leadership mindset can be beneficial and even in some cases save your life, job, and family.

Lower management is a great start despite what most people think. In lower level positions it gives an opportunity to build credibility which can lead to a creative environment. The position of upper management should be to influence their lower management to be innovative. I know what you are thinking and yes it is true. In all cases, not all upper management will do that. One important aspect of being in lower management is to learn but also to show what you learned. If you know an idea or practice that could be of better use than the current one share that with your supervisor or upper management. Lower management positions give the opportunity to excel and show your commitment as a valued employee. This process takes time. IT WILL NOT HAPPEN OVER NIGHT!

Patience, persistence in work, and the willingness to learn will take you further than you think. I was President of an organization called Students in Free Enterprise or S.I.F.E which dealt a lot with entrepreneurship, project management, organizational structure, and leadership. A new member starts off as a project leader. The functions of a project leader are to complete a delegated task from their Vice President or President. The wonderful thing about this position is that it encourages creativity and innovation. In this position, I was able to start out and share ideas that eventually gave momentum to the project. It dealt with environmental sustainability focused on recycling. After serving as project leader for one semester in college, I received a promotion to Vice President of Environmental Sustainability to further the impact of the project. I had the leadership mindset as a project leader. I learned how to develop the ability to follow someone else. I learned how to research information to stay ahead of the game. I learned to offer advice that could be of benefit. What is the key word I want you to take out of leadership mindset? The word is mind. Your mind and brain are totally different. Your brain helps the body function whereas your mind guides your thinking process. Why did I bring this up? You can't develop a leadership mindset without developing your minds thinking process. We must realize even as a follower we should not let others dictate our thinking. Once that happens developing the leadership mindset is not impossible but takes a great deal longer to develop.

 The thinking process is a way to develop your thoughts and use them to be of benefit. One way of developing your thinking process is by reading. Reading is fundamental to gaining knowledge to incorporate into real-life situations. Current events always are useful for statistical information. Reading leads to research. Research is important to have information to back you up. It keeps you ahead and sets you apart from others. Planning and organizing are a part of the thinking process. We must learn to plan what the strategy should be. Then the thoughts must be organized into an action plan. The leadership mindset can take us a long way on the journey to becoming a leader or advance our current leadership capabilities. I want people to understand the importance of thinking for themselves and allowing creativity and innovation to be a part of their work.

Chapter 3: Self-Worth

What is your self-worth? Did you know that you have self-worth? These are the questions I want you to start asking yourself. When a young lady or man is looking for a relationship, they look for compatibility. One of the key aspects of compatibility they look for is someone who has ambitions and goals. Why? That male or female has already determined where they see themselves and want someone with the same mindset. The leadership mindset, which was explained in chapter 2, showed what kind of mindset should be developed. This mindset is equally important for both males and females.

Self-worth is important in identifying your brand identity. Self-worth shows that you are confident in your abilities. I know you have heard "I have been taken advantage of". Most likely these people were not aware of their self-worth. Self-worth shows that you cannot be purchased at a price. The most important aspect of self-worth is knowing that you are valuable to the workforce and others around you. Self-worth sets you apart from others.

How would you like to set your own salary? As a people, our mindset should not be how much we can make per hour but self-worth translates to an ultimate salary. This point is proven by having a solid yet marketable resume. Self-worth is knowing what you stand for and not settling for anything less. Every individual should establish 3 core values about themselves. The purpose of doing this is to evaluate yourself and then define yourself as an individual. To discover what your 3 core values are an individual must ask himself or herself, what are three things that I stand for? These 3 core values should be written down and carried with you wherever you are. You may want to put it in your room, in your wallet or purse, or in your vehicle. Where ever you put it, it should serve as a motivational factor in your life. Also in self-worth, your appearance is key.

First impressions mean everything. You never know nowadays who is watching you. No matter where you are you must be presentable and wear what I like to call Time Appropriate Clothing. It is really vital to know what kind of clothing can be worn to different events or functions. Terminology such as business casual, business attire, casual wear, and so on. an individual should be aware of. Self-worth contributes to brand identity. In order to be a brand, you must know who you are and carry yourself in a way that individuals will recognize and admire. Vision is also a big component of self-worth. Vision is explained more in detail in a later chapter. Always remember if you do not see value in yourself, society will not acknowledge you as an asset.

Chapter 4: Marketing Your Brand

MMAC YOURSELF OUT

I have a developing theory called the Brand Identity. The Brand Identity is composed of marketability, mindset, appearance, and core values (MMAC). The Brand Identity is what you carry with you always. In a wallet, you always should have your driver's license or identification card on you at all times. Brand Identity is no different than marketing yourself. This leads to a question, how do I market myself or your Brand Identity?

There are 8 key marketing tools you need: a resume, business cards, business attire, portfolio, personal mission statement, elevator pitch, professional networking affiliations, and heart. A resume is a marketing tool that shows how valuable you are and the skill you have. Your resume ultimately lets an interviewer know you are an asset. Your resume builds you up as a professional. The resume secretly makes you a better communicator. You as a brand must speak on what your resume displays. Your resume should be no more than 2 pages long. It should include the following: professional summary, accomplishments, professional skills, employment history, education, computer skills, and any professional memberships that you have. Make sure to get your guidance from someone who you respect to assist in the process.

Business cards are something, some may argue, high school or college students, do not need yet. I advise you to get business cards. There are multiple resources that offer business cards at inexpensive rates. The most popular choice is vistaprint.com. Your business cards, like your resume, are a reflection of yourself. If the option is given, get a professional picture on your business cards. Every time a business card is handed out it is less likely the individual will forget you. Make sure you have a simple email address, reachable phone number, address, and other beneficial information if available (such as a professional website, blog, and your personal mission statement considering it is short). I always keep business cards on me because you never know who in life you will meet and where. Also, it is a way to impress that young lady or man you want to impress. Remember though, on a serious note your business cards are a way of promoting your brand.

In order for the business world to take people seriously, an image must be maintained. Business attire is something that establishes the outward brand. Depending on what career choice you make most will require business attire or at least business casual. These terms are important to know as emphasized earlier. Business casual varies among industry standards. Also when you dress up it gives you a sense of confidence. Every person should have a business casual and professional attire. Business casual consist of a nice solid button up dress shirt (with the collar open or tie depending on your preference), solid pair of dress pants. In business casual a blazer is optional. Your shoes should also be a solid conservative color (black or dark blue) and should always be shined. Socks should follow a similar color pattern of your dress pants or shoes. The color of your belt should always match the color of your shoes. Females wear a blouse, a dress or skirt at knee-length or below, a tailored blazer, and dress shoes that cover all or most of the foot. Our professional attire for the males would be a conservative suit (dark blue or grey), dress shirt (white most of the time), belt that matches the same color of shoes, and black or navy blue shoes shined. For a female, a dark pant suit, hosiery, and pumps (closed toe with a heel).

The last thing to note is to know when to wear the right attire. Business casual you typically will wear to a company party, daily work attire (as some companies will permit), and business lunch meetings. Professional attire should be worn in an office environment, during workshops/conferences, and to a job interview. It is important to remember that the way we dress has a factor in our success.

The next important item for success is your own unique portfolio. Your portfolio descriptively shares your accomplishments. It is good to keep all articles about you, your resume, meaningful projects/papers in your portfolio. Your portfolio is YOU. It tells your story. In there, you will find where you have been, what you have done, your skillsets and hobbies, accomplishments, and so. Think of your portfolio as an extension of your resume. They both have the same content but the portfolio expands on whatever is on the resume. It is important to have one especially when in a job interview. Personally, for myself, I find it most useful when providing examples of the work I have done. When that is shared, it helps the employers see you have supportive examples of how you can contribute to the job/career.

Every business must have a mission statement and a vision statement. A mission statement will share who the business will be serving and how it will be done. A vision statement shares the impact and direction over the course of time. So it tends to be more statistical. In the vision statement, it highlights specific numbers of who will be reached in a time frame. It may also highlight how much the business look to make over a certain period of time. I am still keeping you in the mindset of you being Me, Inc. So how do mission and vision relate to you as an individual? Just like a business, we as individuals should have a mission to accomplish and a vision to enroll people. Enrollment is directly influencing a person to support. Having a vision and mission statement takes your brand to a whole different level. When people see you have a mission and vision they can see potential in developing a relationship with you. According to Forbes.com, there are 4 questions companies ask themselves to develop their mission statements.

1. What do we do?

2. How do we do it?

3. Whom do we do it for?

4. What value are we bringing?

Now, this format has served many major corporations. Let's translate this into something even more powerful for you. All we have to do is swap out one word for another. That is swapping out we for I. Let's try again and see.

1. What do I do?

2. How do I do it?

3. Whom do I do it for?

4. What value am I bringing?

By answering these questions, you have the necessary tools to pull together a great mission statement that will draw people to you. Let me use myself for example. I use marketing and leadership techniques to motivate young people to become leaders. I share marketing and leadership techniques through speaking engagements. I am teaching skillsets for young people to follow their dreams which will translate to entrepreneurship. Now let's pull these answers altogether. My personal mission statement is I am a young marketing professional sharing leadership and branding techniques with youth in result making dreams truly a reality. Make sure to take what you learned and make your personal mission statement. This really gives you an opportunity to learn about yourself as well.

If you were in an elevator and you only had from the time you got on to the time you got off to describe your passion in life, what would you say? Often time we drag our vision out longer than needed. The average length of an elevator pitch should be no longer than 30 seconds. For example, my elevator pitch is I am a young professional using social media marketing to create brand awareness.

The purpose of an elevator pitch is to quickly gain the interest of an individual as a gateway to a conversation. Many elevator pitches lead to strategic partnerships and business startups. Your elevator pitch is designed to quickly share a vision. Once interest is created it allows an opening to provide descriptive details about your vision. When was the last time you were at an event shaking hands with either like-minded individuals or others that are industry leaders? If it has been more than a couple months, it is time to start back up. Professional networking allows an open free community to learn about other businesses and promote your own. Why is this important? Other business professionals may be a good fit to collaborate with or as a reliable reference. I learned the value of being a master networker through ENACTUS (an entrepreneurship organization). I valued the experience of networking that led to corporate and world leaders. The key professional relationships will come from the basics.

1. Be 100% authentic!

    a. Your values should always be expressed. Share your vision and why it matters.

2. Think relationship!

   a. Business partnerships and collaborations come after developing a relationship. Develop trust and honesty with the individual you speak with. The relationship starts after the first 3 emails to the individual. The business card does not create the relationship the dialogue afterward does.

3. Your Story!

   a. Always share how you got to where you are now. Your story is the emotional key to opening up the success door. People are sold not on what you accomplish but the story behind the accomplishment. What makes you unique compared to others?

4. Business Cards.

   a. Always have business cards available to give if someone is interested in connecting with you. Your business card must relate to you and your vision. Just like your resume a business card is also a representation of yourself.

When marketing yourself, you are being a self-motivated leader. Self-motivated leaders have a heart. Your heart is admitting and taking action of the well-being of others. One time I gave a speech on Spiritual Leadership: The 3 Key Elements to Leadership. The three keys elements I briefly spoke on were brand, love, and service. A leader with a heart must have all three. Having a heart is owning your worth which translate into realizing your brand identity. Being a brand comes with assuming the risk. Your brand is like a corporation or brand name product. Any successful company or product came with risk. Accepting risks while claiming your vision makes you a brand. Through adversity, a business or corporation develop their heart (mission and vision statements). They are formed through what love they found in their branding process, it is implemented through mission and vision through overcoming obstacles (the fulfillment factor).

Every business creates their love for humanity after their branding process. Love is the glue that holds leadership together. We cannot be an effective leader if we do not love. Love is not always agreement but acceptance. Every leader that shows acceptance gains respect. Acceptance is not of the leader but to those that follow. As leaders, we must accept and appreciate the qualities of those that are different and empower them to be effective.

As leaders, we must have the heart of service. Typically, leaders that have a heart of service excel far more than those who want a title. Service comes from the inside and is displayed on the outside. Most leaders have a story dear to their heart that causes love and love translate into service. The reason service is so powerful in leadership is because outreach is visionary. Imagine this, if you only empower those in your organization to do stuff for themselves, the impact is going to be limited to only your surroundings. If empowerment is experienced together in the community impact is unlimited to the world. I want you to think about what you stand for in life and events that influenced them. You got it! Good, now you are equipped to serve those who are being affected by an unconnected society. We must position ourselves as solutionist.

Chapter 5: The Mindset of Learning

Leaders never stop learning. As a matter of fact, the strongest leader's practice self-study. There are many ways of doing so like attending conferences, obtaining mentors in his or her industry, or getting certified or licensed to become an expert in his or her industry. What are you doing right now to advance yourself in your major, business, or hobby? If you haven't thought about it, it is now the time to start thinking about it. What you don't know now, is that you want to be known as an "expert or specialist" in your industry. They constantly practice and apply what they learn in action. Through doing this, you know what works and what things can be improved. Being an expert or specialist simply is someone who learns, practice, apply and evaluate. Your mindset determines your direction in life. If you have the mindset of success you will succeed. If you have the mindset of doubt you will not advance. Where is your mindset? We all from time to time need a mindset transformation. Mindset transformation all begins with letting go of what's impossible and accepting that anything is possible. We must believe in something. Let us begin with believing we are destined for greatness.

A big part of learning is not being afraid to make mistakes. Now, even in being positive in our thoughts we still may make mistakes. Mistakes are the double lines on the road. Once you see the lines on the road you know what side of the road to be on. The key thing is getting back on track and not turning around. Learning gives you an element of power. This power can be used for good or bad. It is important to use the power of learning to help empower those that need it. Never keep learning to yourself. If you cook a Thanksgiving meal for family and friends but do not invite them to partake in the dinner with you it's pointless. Don't have your learning being pointless but meaningful.

Also as a leader, we must focus on experimental learning. We must learn to take risks and try new things. If we continue doing the same things, we will never produce new and fresh results. In the age we live in, we learn to become innovators. Why? We must learn to compete globally. Innovators are the ones that will always be ahead of the game. One of the biggest things I learned was you have to stretch yourself in order to have the biggest revelation about yourself. When you can accomplish something on your own that is uncomfortable that is when you know you are learning and advancing.

Who are you learning from? This question plays a key role in learning. You must learn from those who have been where you were or those that have a vested interest in your future. These people necessarily don't even have to be in your field. Listen to the motivational material to keep your adrenaline going. People like pastors, educators, motivational speakers, business and political leaders all had to start from somewhere. Everyone has unique things you can learn from. Now what kind of things should I be learning? The best kind of learning is development, career advancement, time management, organizing, and so on. These learning methods are all must have to be an effective leader.

Why are learning and knowledge a priceless possession? You give learning and knowledge the power by action and no one can take it from you. That is why you should never take education for granted. Also, I encourage you to self-study more. Find out what your passion is and on your own time study and perfect it. No matter whether classifying yourself as a leader or entrepreneur self-study is key to accelerating your journey.

Chapter 6: Credibility: Your ID and Social Security Number

Every day we must have our ID or driver's license card and social security number memorized. Why? Each day we never know what is going to happen. We don't know if we are going to get pulled over by the police for speeding or have to validate who we are if an emergency happens. So we must carry it at all times. This is a means to identify who we are and have proof to back it. Credibility is no different. Our credibility comes from the actions we implement, the professionalism we use, and the spirit we give off. Our credibility represents the value we can provide to others. As a credible individual, we must be able to provide a track record that we can be valuable. Credibility starts at home. Parents train their kids from being little to being credible. Small things such as doing homework on your own, being there for a friend's birthday party, or performing your chores without being told builds credibility. In the business world and as a brand, we should always have our credibility showing. Therefore, we must always let our light shine among those we come in contact with.

How should we gain credibility? First, we must first rise to the occasion. Opportunities are plentiful but we must seize them to have a chance to be credible. Let yourself be known to gain opportunities to serve and offer your talents and abilities. Second, open communication helps to keep those who you serve aware of your progress. Open communication makes it easy for individuals to know you can come to them in the case of need or progress. Third, consistency is a trait that shows no matter what the situation you will stick with it until it is done. This shows you have a strong sense of reliability. Fourth, the presentation is key to presenting any work that you have done. Any work and task submitted should be done with excellence and professionalism. Fifth and finally, follow up is crucial. Think of this as building a network of connections. Individuals you build relationships with will become colleagues, strategic partners, or even supporters. You always want to follow up not only on your current task but future projects. The great thing is that you never know when your connection will offer another project or sponsor a project of yours.

Chapter 7: Legacy Building

You have one life, to fulfill one vision, to leave one legacy.

What do you want to leave for your family? What do you want to be remembered for? What mark do you want to leave the world? These are some questions that we must all ask ourselves. We are all put on this earth for a purpose. Our purpose is what drives us to build our legacy.

I would define legacy as the mark left behind for the betterment of community, family, and mankind. We all want to in some way or another to provide for a family and leave something behind. Leaving something behind is bigger than just a $100,000 life insurance policy. Legacy is bigger than financial perks. Legacy is a cause that is embedded so deep in your heart that you lose sleep over it.

In order to start legacy building, you must have your kit available. The first thing in your kit should be the purpose. We are not on this earth to occupy it but to have dominion over it. Every person on this earth believe it or not has a purpose within even if it is not activated. You must determine what your purpose is. What is something that you love doing or are really talented in that you can share with the world? I want you to take some time and actually write that down. This will be helpful in creating some clarity on where your focus should be in your legacy building. Every purpose that a person has should be clear. Remember purpose drives legacy.

The second tool in your kit is a vision. You know your purpose by this point and now you need to paint a clear picture. Your vision is a transparent means of where you see yourself going. A vision helps relay to others how your vision will have an impact. Vision has long-term potential and will have sustainability. Sustainability ensures that your fulfilled vision will still be in the hearts of many for years and decades to come. Your vision should consist of family, ownership, and service/scholarship. The final part of a vision is actually making your vision statement for yourself. Your vision statement should include all 3 of the following elements above. My vision statement is creating fulfillment through youth empowerment while displaying a generational seed for the family lineage.

The third tool is motivation. Money is low, work seems unbearable, and on top of that people are doubting your course of direction. Sounds scary right? That is where motivation comes in. Motivation is what keeps you hungry and relentless in the face of adversity. Use your motivation as your fuel for the fire. The fact of the matter is there are others you are competing with but your motivation sets you apart from anyone else. Know that you are unique. Pressing on when you don't know the way and other doubt you is motivation. I want you to close your eyes and think of the person who influenced you the most so far in life directly (such as a grandmother, mom, dad, etc.). Do you have that person? Now, image all they've done for you, all you want to do for them, and how smart you are willing to work to make sure you never let them down. Do you have it? Congratulations, you now have the formula for motivation.

The last and final tool is service. You have motivation now but now it is time for your course of action. Whether you have a business idea, nonprofit, an aspiring author, always ask yourself how I can benefit my community for a better cause. I knew an executive once that said, "The only way to become successful is by making other people successful." The key to having a successful project or business other than profit is having fun, creativity, and serving others in the process. With these tools, you will reach your final destination, legacy.

SPECIAL DEDICATION

GONE BUT NOT FORGOTTEN

Josephine Johnson (Grandmother)

Mr. Jack Spinner (My Adopted Grandfather)

SPECIAL THANKS

Special Thanks to all family and friends.

Special Acknowledgement to Chestley Talley

(Leadership Mentor), and my parents

Pearl and Winston Johnson

SPEAKING ENGAGEMENT

One Life, One, Vision, One Legacy Tour

Through

Do you have youth that needs direction, guidance, and principles to follow in and out of the classroom?

Contact Us

Expression Enterprise

expressionenterprise@gmail.com

www.expressionenterprise.org

www.ingramcontent.com/pod-product-compliance
Lightning Source LLC
Chambersburg PA
CBHW061233180526
45170CB00003B/1275